Thank You FOR BEING A Nurse!

Keepsake Gift Book

A Gift For:

____

From:

____

To know even one life has breathed easier because you have lived. This is to have succeeded.

—*Bessie Anderson Stanley*

In every gentle touch and
every word of encouragement,
you bring hope and dignity.

Let us never consider ourselves finished nurses. We must be learning all of our lives.

—Florence Nightingale, British social reformer and founder of modern nursing

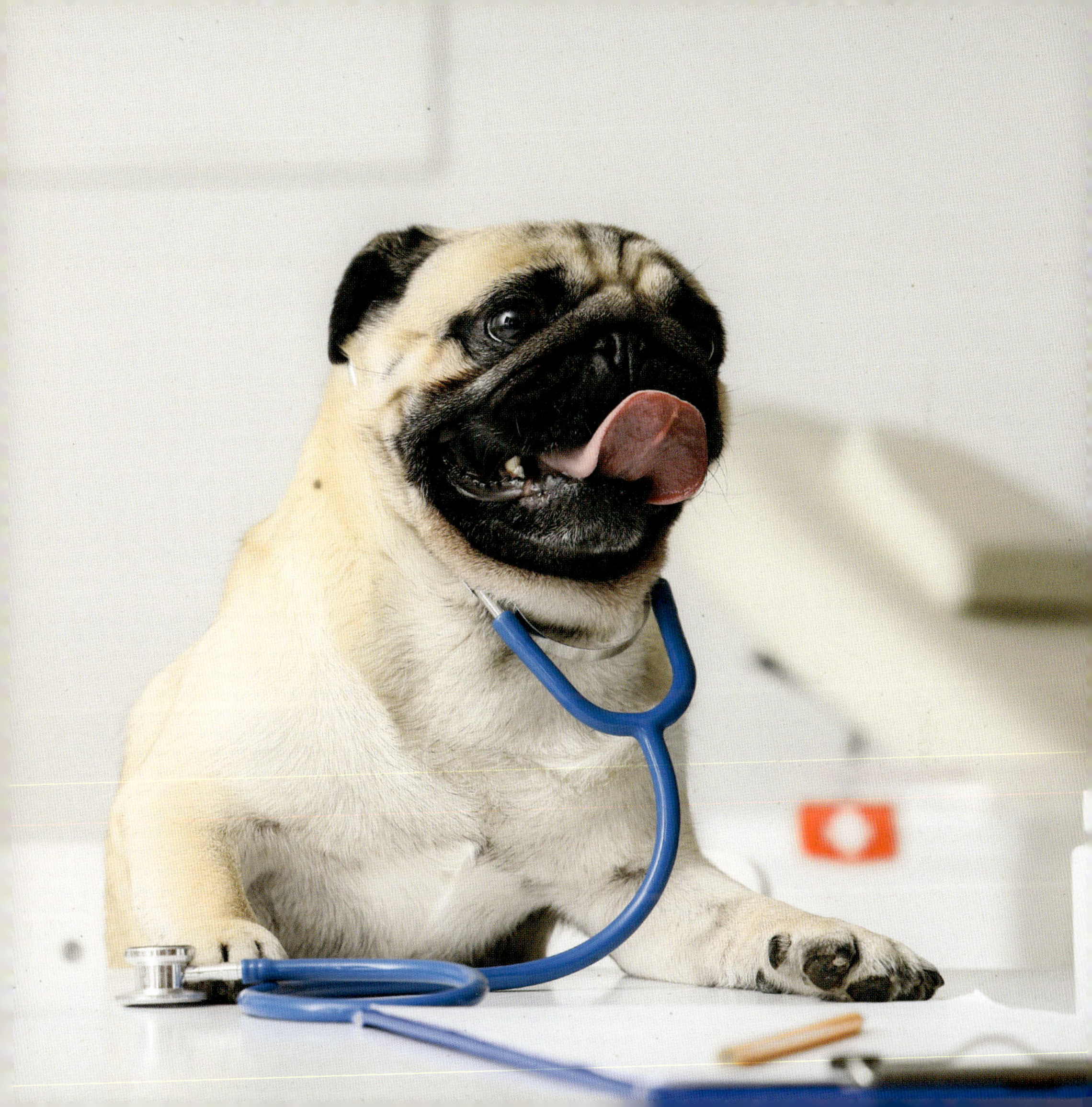

*A cheerful heart is good medicine,
but a crushed spirit dries up the bones.*

—Proverbs 17:22

To do what nobody else will do, a way that nobody else can do, in spite of all we go through; that is to be a nurse.

—Rawsi Williams, BSN, RN, CQRMS-LTC, American nurse, attorney, and veteran

We've been wrong about what our job is in medicine. We think our job is to ensure health and survival. But really it is larger than that. It is to enable well-being.

—Atul Gawande, American surgeon and author of *Being Mortal*

Your compassion, strength, and dedication are gifts that bring healing far beyond medicine.

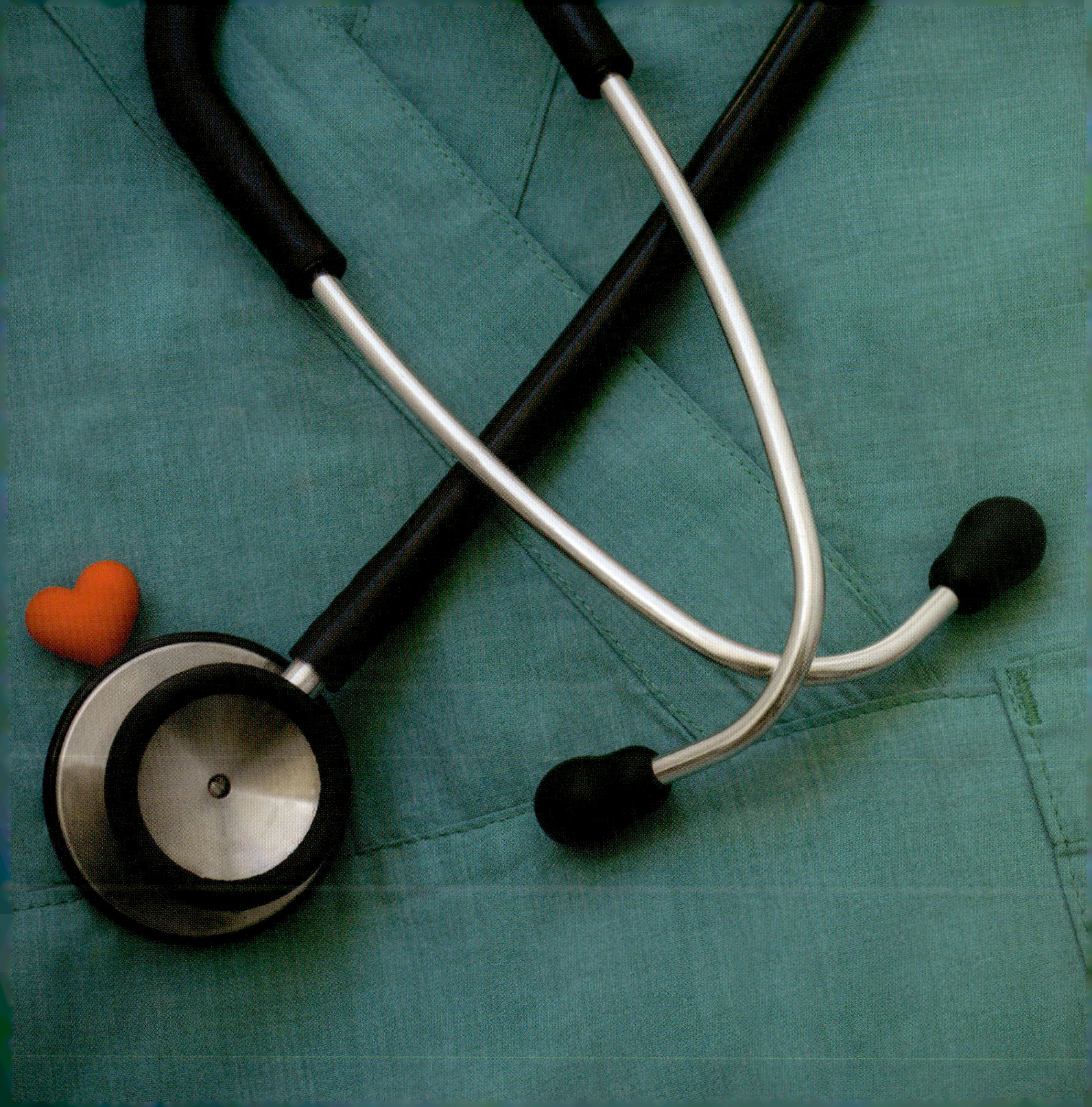

Too often we underestimate the power of a touch, a smile, a kind word, a listening ear, an honest compliment, or the smallest act of caring, all of which have the potential to turn a life around.

—*Leo Buscaglia*

Thank you for being the gentle rainbow that follows the storm—a sign that brighter days are ahead.

It would not be possible to praise nurses too highly.

—*Stephen Ambrose*

*You comfort with your presence,
heal with your care, and inspire
with your unwavering spirit.*

Nurses are there when the last breath is taken, and nurses are there when the first breath is taken. Although it is more enjoyable to celebrate the birth, it is just as important to comfort in death.

—Christine Bell,
American nurse practitioner

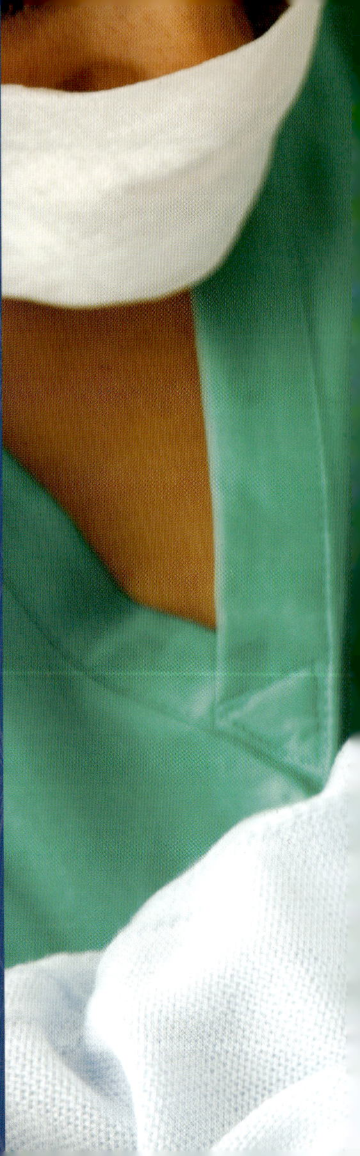

Thank you for being the light in the darkest times, and for helping others find their way back to health.

Thank you for being the steady hands and kind heart we all need in our most vulnerable moments.

In every act of kindness, we nurture the seeds of hope.

—Clara Barton, American nurse and founder of the American Red Cross

Thank you for bringing
comfort in tough times.
Your care makes even
the worst day better.

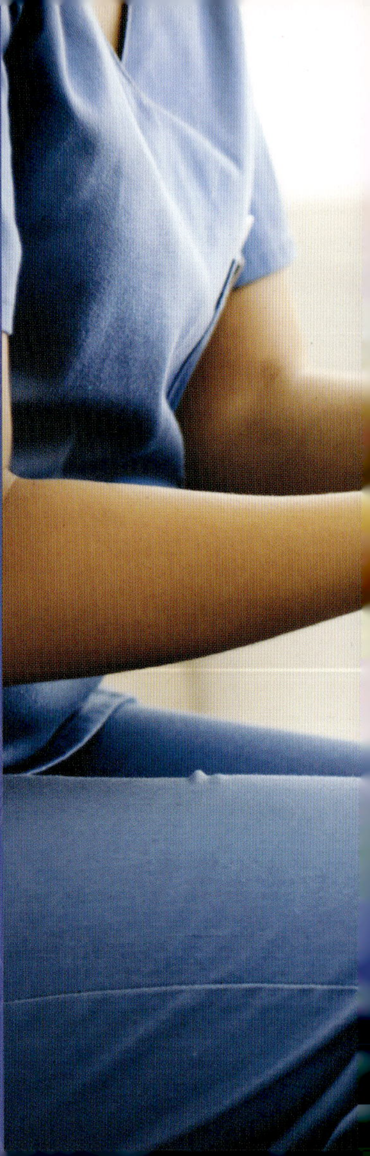

As a nurse, we have the opportunity to heal the mind, soul, heart, and body of our patients. They may forget your name, but they will never forget how you made them feel.

—Maya Angelou

You give so much of yourself
so others can feel safe, seen,
and supported—thank you.

Nurses are the hospitality of the hospital.

—Carrie Latet

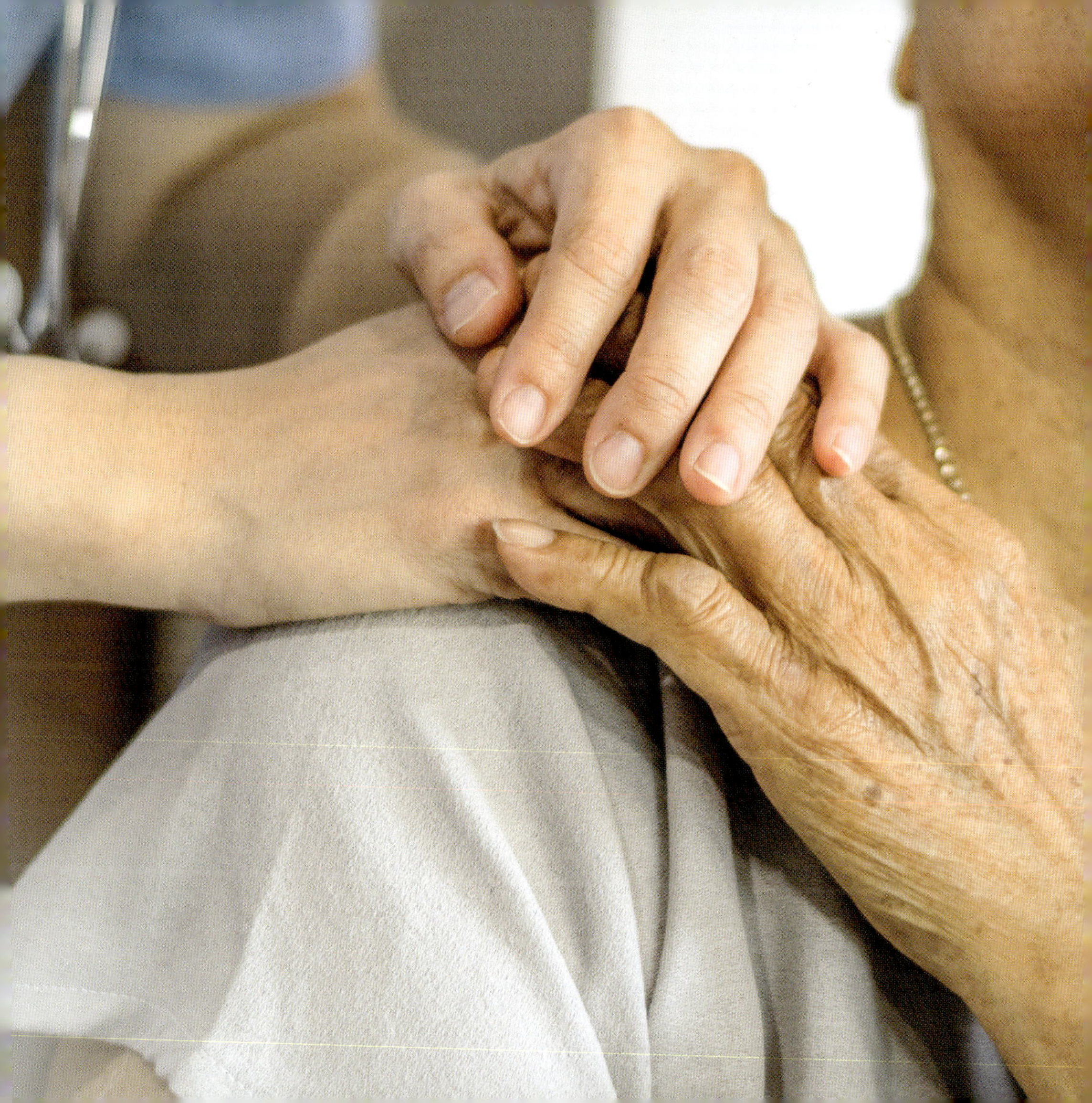

There is no greater contribution than to help the weak.

—Walter Reuther

Life is not easy for any of us. But what of that? We must have perseverance and, above all, confidence in ourselves. We must believe that we are gifted for something, and that this thing must be attained.

—*Marie Curie*

Your tireless care and quiet sacrifices do not go unnoticed. You are truly a hero.

With care and patience, people may accomplish things which, to an indolent person, would appear impossible.

—*Dorothea Dix, American nurse and advocate for mental illness*

Our fingerprints don't fade
from the lives we touch.

—*Judy Blume*

It takes courage to care about
people as much as you do,
and to show up every day.
Thank you for being brave.

Don't forget you are a nurse.
Don't forget the human interaction,
that's what helps people.

—Loretta C. Ford, American nurse and co-founder of the first nurse practitioner program

You heal not just with your skills, but with your heart, and that makes all the difference.

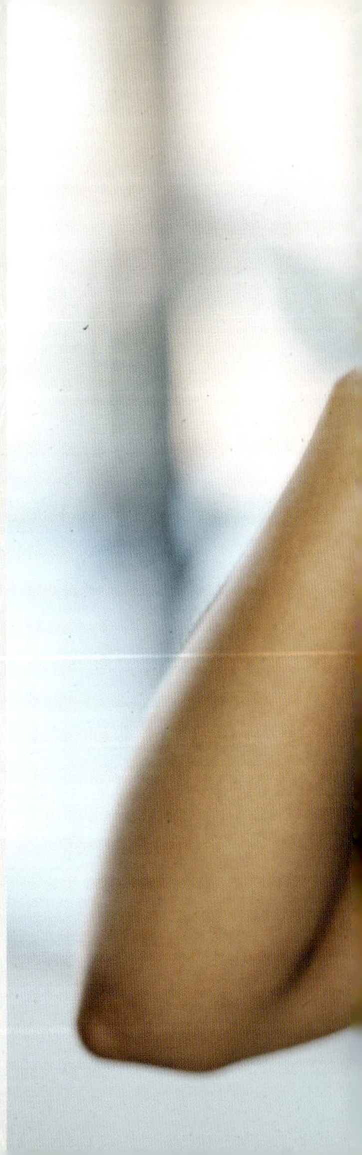

The nurse is temporarily the consciousness of the unconscious . . . the leg of the amputee, the eyes of the newly blind . . . knowledge and confidence for the young mother, a voice for those too weak, and so on.

—Virginia Henderson, American nurse, author, and researcher

Each day you show up
with grace, courage, and
compassion—and for that,
we are deeply grateful.

Your profession is not what brings home your weekly paycheck, your profession is what you're put here on earth to do, with such passion and such intensity that it becomes spiritual in calling.

—*Vincent van Gogh*

The world is better, kinder, and more hopeful because of nurses like you—thank you for everything.

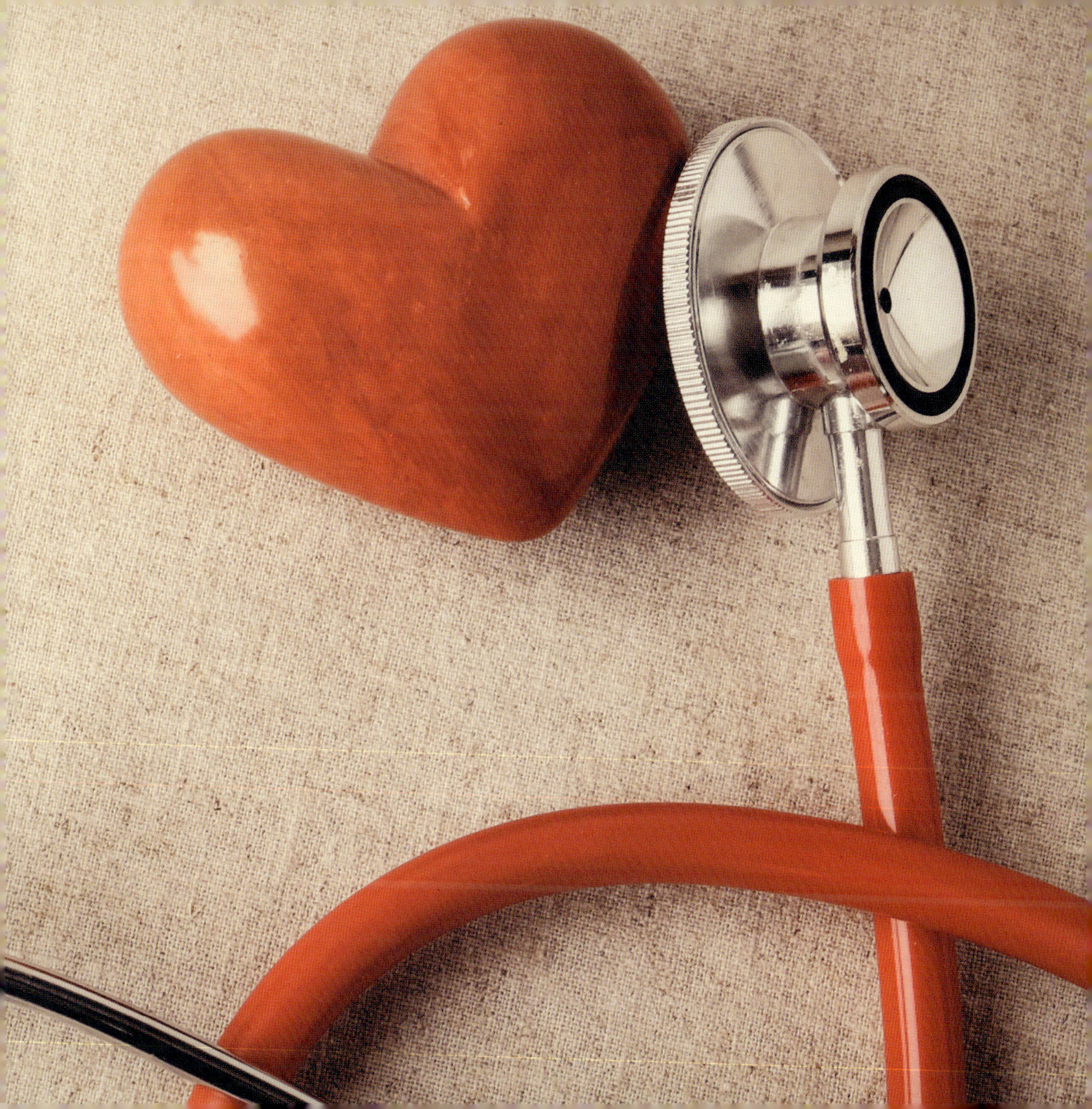

Images from Shutterstock.com: LedyX (cover); TopFlatShots (3); PeopleImages.com – Yuri A (5, 11, 33, 55); Pixel-Shot (7); Ground Picture (8–9); Esgoty (11); icemanphotos (12–13, 46–47); Kalanchoe (15); Skoles (16–17); Sergei25 (18–19); BlurryMe (20–21); Bk87 (23); Air Images (24–25); Kub The Shadow Simple Man (26–27); Guitarfoto (29); tongo51 (30–31); Svitlana Hulko (35); GolubaPhoto (36–37); Prostock-Studio (39); Dmytro Zinkevych (40–41); KieferPix (43); emerald media (44–45); galihsputro (46–47); SewCreamStudio (48–49); EB Adventure Photography (50–51); David Gyung (53); Paul Nash (57); lenetstan (59); Aleksei Leonoff (61).

ISBN 978-1-4971-0603-1

Library of Congress Control Number: 2025917315

To learn more about the other great books from Fox Chapel Publishing, or to find a retailer near you, call toll-free at 800-457-9112 or visit us at *www.FoxChapelPublishing.com*.

We are always looking for talented authors.
To submit an idea, please send a brief inquiry to acquisitions@foxchapelpublishing.com.

Or write to:
Fox Chapel Publishing
903 Square Street
Mount Joy, PA 17552

Printed in China
First printing

MIX
Paper | Supporting responsible forestry
FSC® C016973